Música Latina para dos 3

5 Intermediate Piano Duets That Celebrate Latin American Styles

Latin America, including Central and South America, has produced some of the most captivating music in history! Perhaps it is because this music is a product of many cultures. Africans, Europeans, and indigenous people have come together to create unique musical styles that use rhythmic syncopations, colorful harmonies, and mesmerizing melodies.

In the *Música Latina* series, students experience the rhythms, styles, and musical characteristics of Latin American music while exploring the history and culture of this part of the world. Each duet begins with short rhythm exercises in the *primo* and *secondo* that prepare students for the rhythm patterns featured in the piece. A brief description of each title helps spark the performers' imaginations. Through the music in Book 3, intermediate students will celebrate the sounds of Latin music—*Música Latina*.

Wynn-Anne Rossi

Contents

Alfred Music
P.O. Box 10003
Van Nuys, CA 91410-0003
alfred.com

ISBN-10: 1-4706-2305-6
ISBN-13: 978-1-4706-2305-0
Cover Illustration:
Mexican-themed pattern: © Shutterstock.com / mattasbestos

Viaje al Salto Ángel

"Journey to Angel Falls"

Angel Falls, in the heart of Venezuela, is the highest uninterrupted waterfall in the world. In the local Pemon language, it is called "Kerepakupai Vená," meaning "waterfall of the deepest place."

Rhythm Workshop

Tap rhythm 3x daily.

mm. 20–22

Secondo

Wynn-Anne Rossi

Viaje al Salto Ángel

"Journey to Angel Falls"

Angel Falls, in the heart of Venezuela, is the highest uninterrupted waterfall in the world. In the local Pemon language, it is called "Kerepakupai Vená," meaning "waterfall of the deepest place."

Rhythm Workshop

Tap rhythm 3x daily.

mm. 15–17

Primo

Wynn-Anne Rossi

With energetic anticipation! ($\bullet$ = 108)

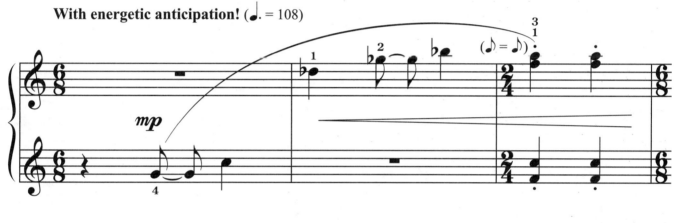

Nova bossa nova

"New Bossa Nova"

In Brazil, the word "bossa" is old-fashioned slang for something that is done
with a natural flair. The bossa nova style
evolved from samba. It is less percussive
but more harmonically complex.

Secondo

Wynn-Anne Rossi

Nova bossa nova

"New Bossa Nova"

In Brazil, the word "bossa" is old-fashioned slang for something that is done with a natural flair. The bossa nova style evolved from samba. It is less percussive but more harmonically complex.

Rhythm Workshop

Tap rhythm 3x daily.

mm. 22–23

Primo

Wynn-Anne Rossi

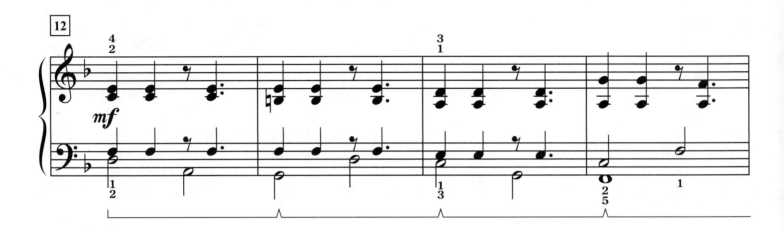

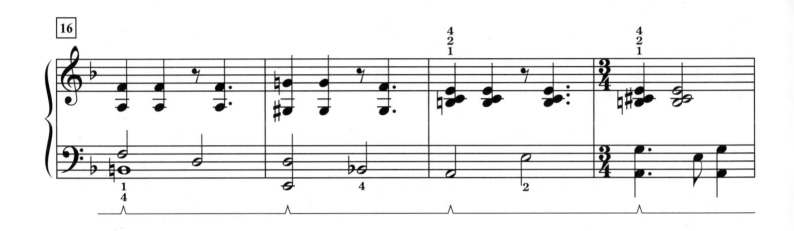

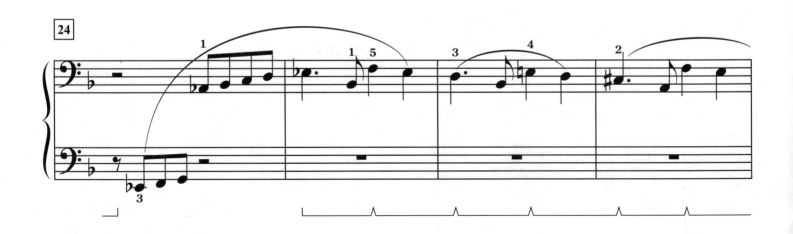

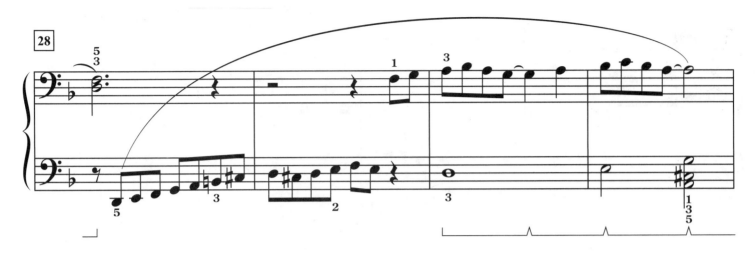

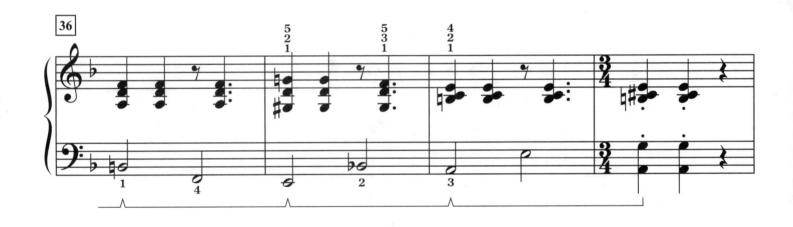

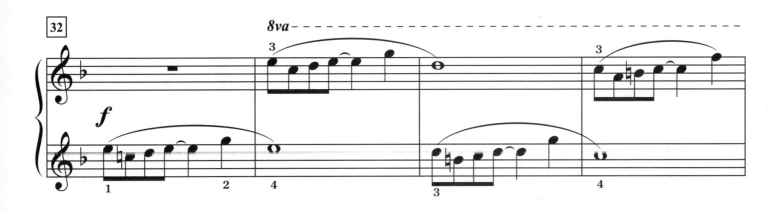

Volcán Santa María

"Saint Maria Volcano"

No trip to Guatemala is complete without a hike to the top of the volcano. The
view from Santa Maria is breathtaking!
When night falls, the sky is filled with
the wonder of bright stars and galaxies.

Rhythm Workshop

Tap rhythm 3x daily.

mm. 17–18

Secondo

Wynn-Anne Rossi

Mysteriously (♩ = 100)

Volcán Santa María

"Saint Maria Volcano"

No trip to Guatemala is complete without a hike to the top of the volcano. The view from Santa Maria is breathtaking! When night falls, the sky is filled with the wonder of bright stars and galaxies.

Rhythm Workshop

Tap rhythm 3x daily.

mm. 13–14

Primo

Wynn-Anne Rossi

Mysteriously (♩ = 100)

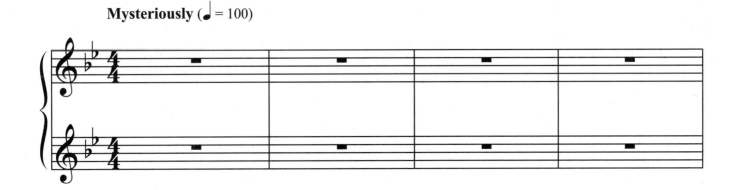

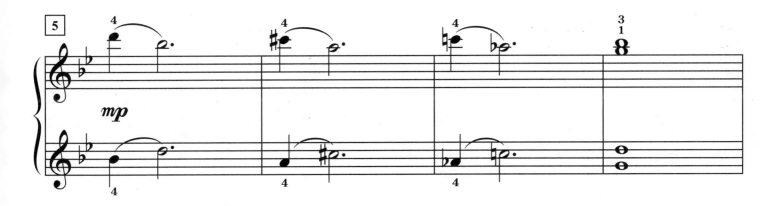

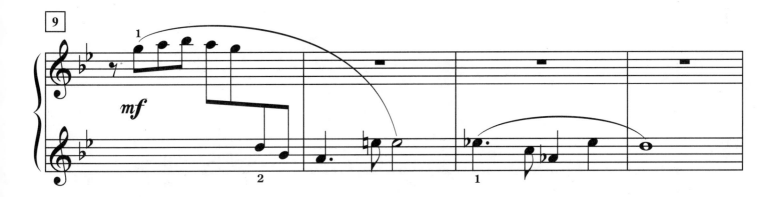

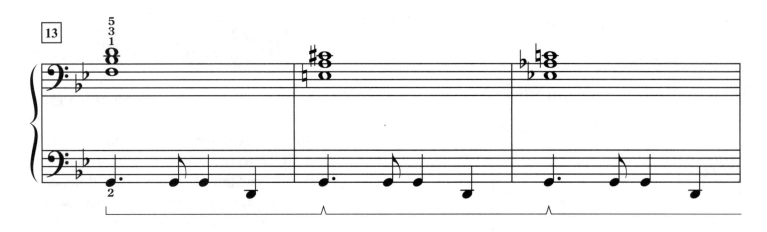

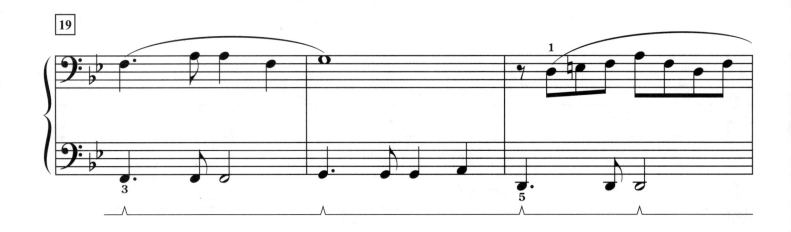

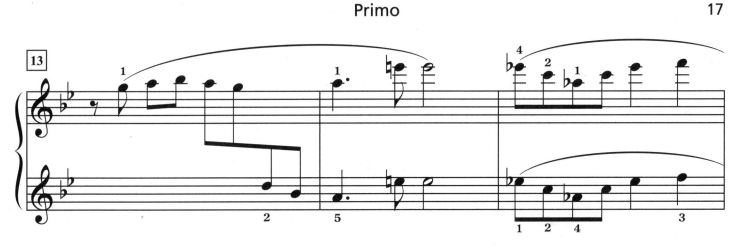

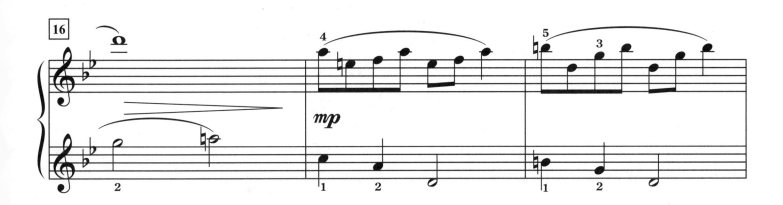

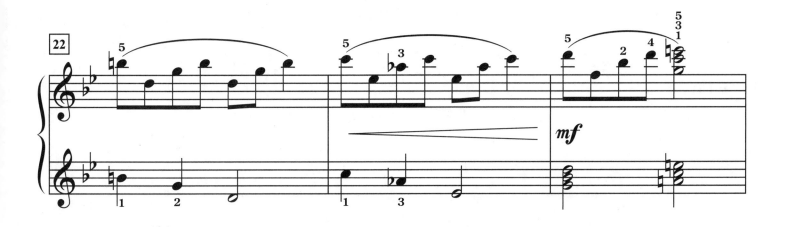

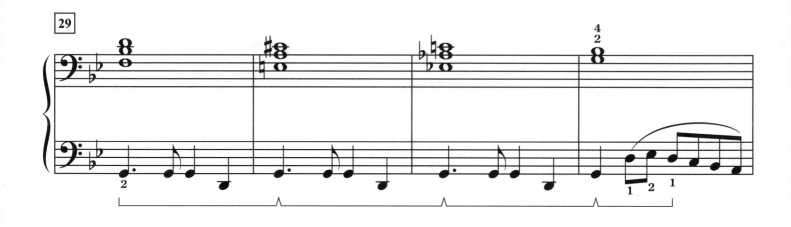

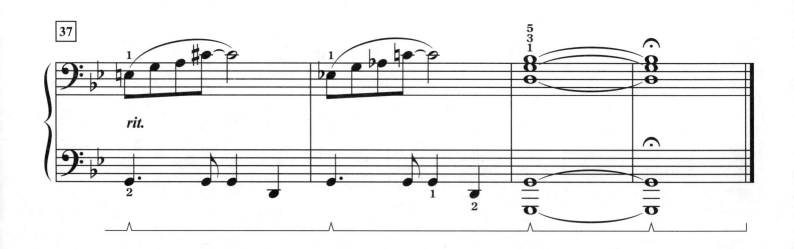

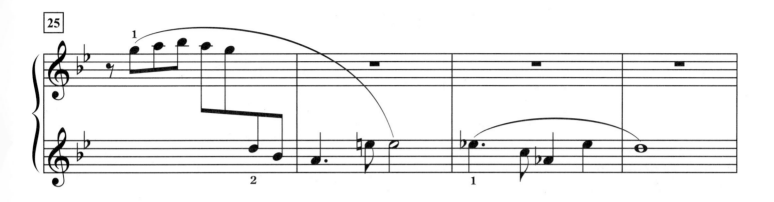

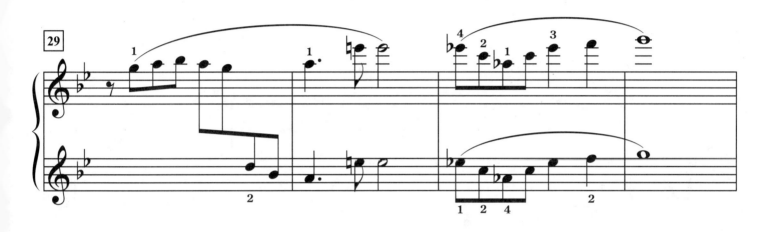

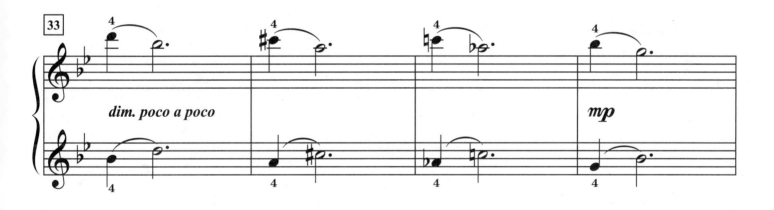

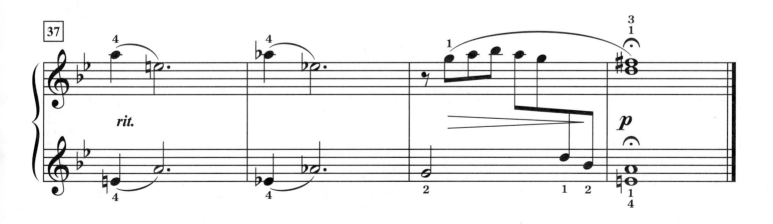

Una rumba en mi corazón

"A Rumba in My Heart"

Rumba emerged in Cuba in the 1880s when slavery was abolished. It served as a form of expression for those who had been oppressed. It is a combination of Afro-Cuban music, dance, and poetry.

Rhythm Workshop

Tap rhythm 3x daily.

mm. 4–6

Secondo

Wynn-Anne Rossi

Una rumba en mi corazón

"A Rumba in My Heart"

Rumba emerged in Cuba in the 1880s when slavery was abolished. It served as a form of expression for those who had been oppressed. It is a combination of Afro-Cuban music, dance, and poetry.

Rhythm Workshop

Tap rhythm 3x daily.

mm. 4–6

Primo

Wynn-Anne Rossi

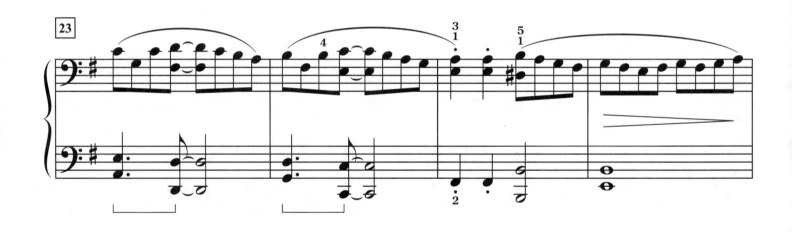

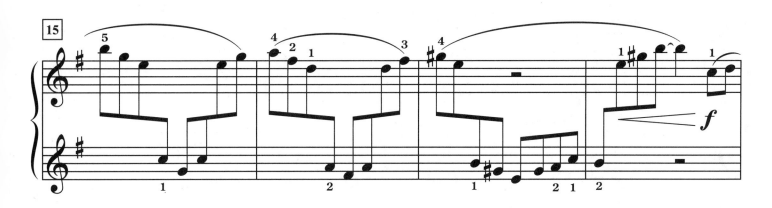

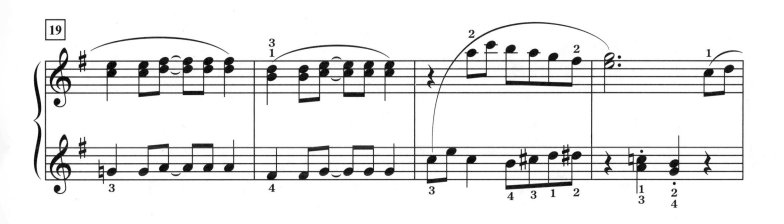

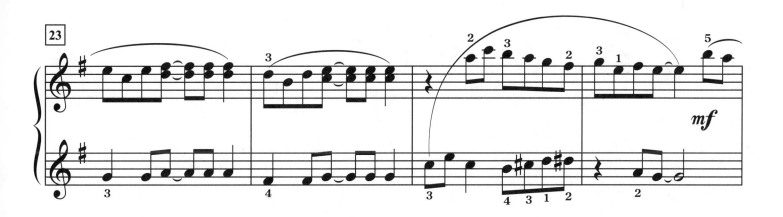

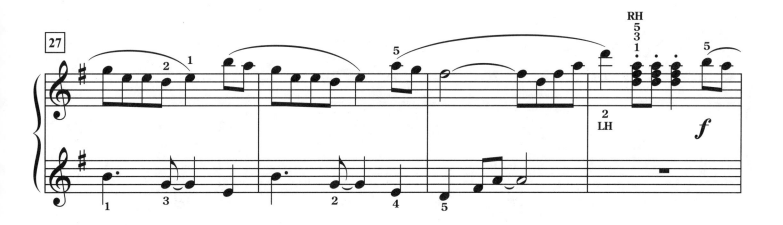

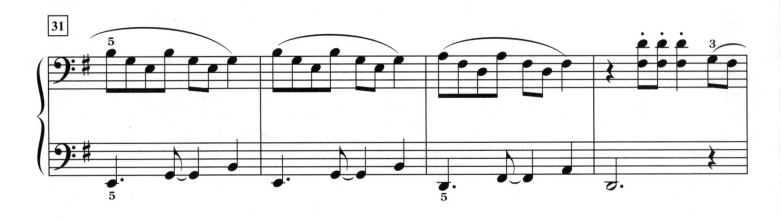

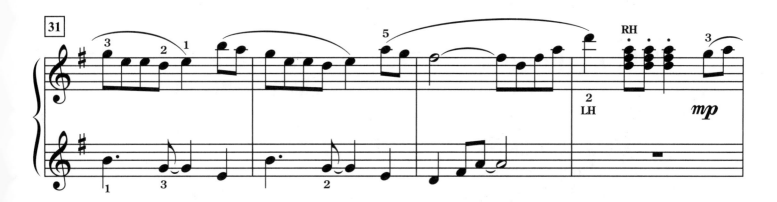

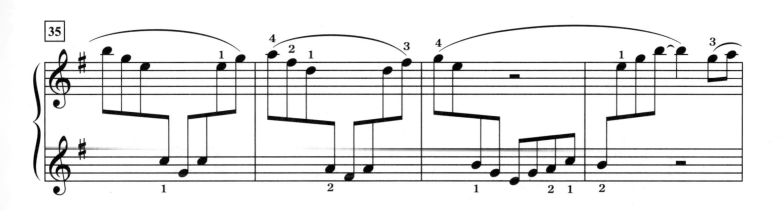

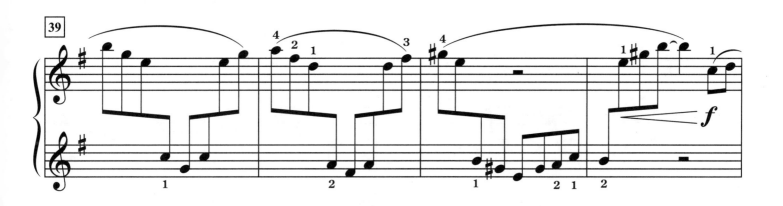

To my friend Peggy, who always captures the beat!

Celebración mambo

"Mambo Celebration"

Mambo means "conversation with the Gods" in Kikongo, a language formerly spoken by African slaves in Cuba. The mambo music and dance style began in Cuba and developed in Mexico.

Rhythm Workshop

Tap rhythm 3x daily.

mm. 9–10

Secondo

Twice the spice! ($\textbf{d} = 72$)

Wynn-Anne Rossi

Rhythm Workshop

Tap rhythm 3x daily.

mm. 17–18

To my friend Peggy, who always captures the beat!

Celebración mambo

"Mambo Celebration"

Mambo means "conversation with the Gods" in Kikongo, a language formerly spoken by African slaves in Cuba. The mambo music and dance style began in Cuba and developed in Mexico.

Primo

Wynn-Anne Rossi

Twice the spice! ($\bf d$ = 72)

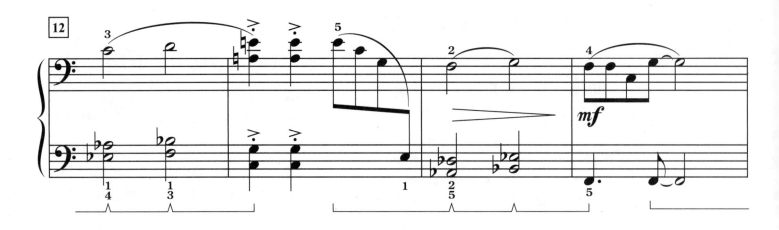

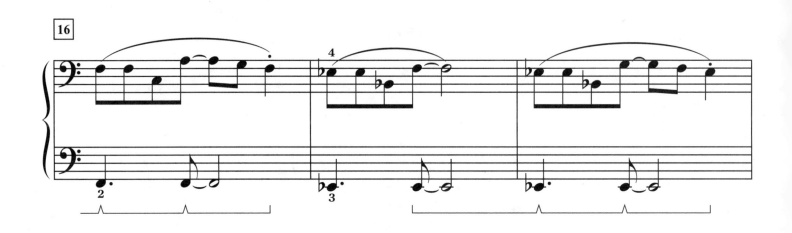

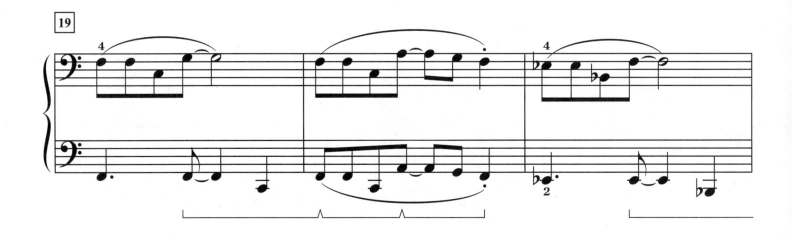

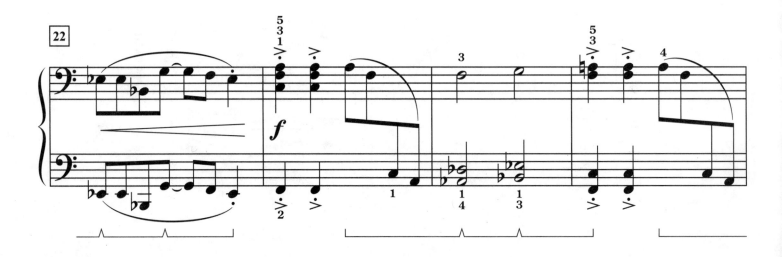

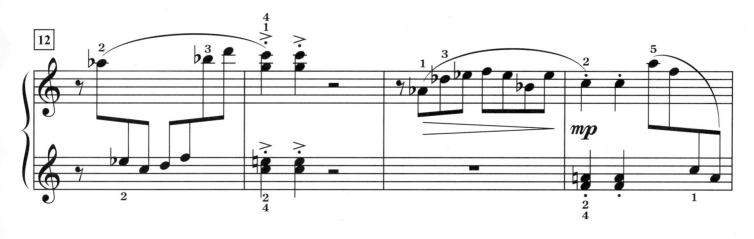

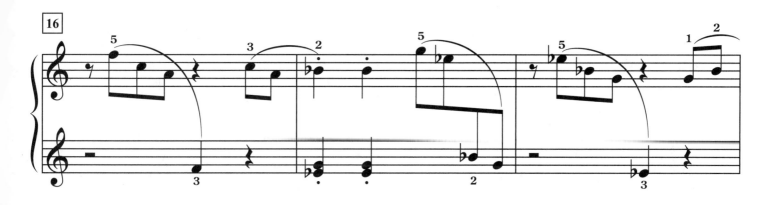

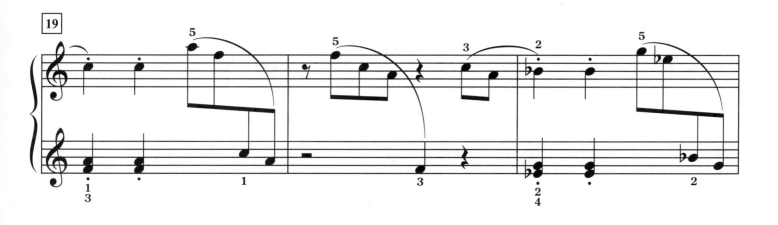

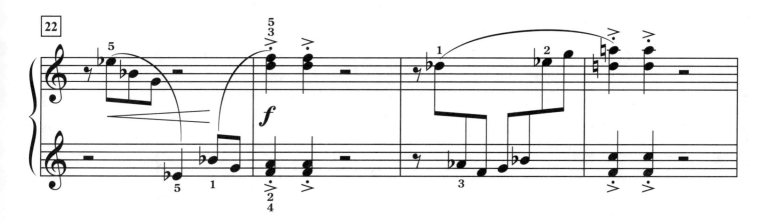

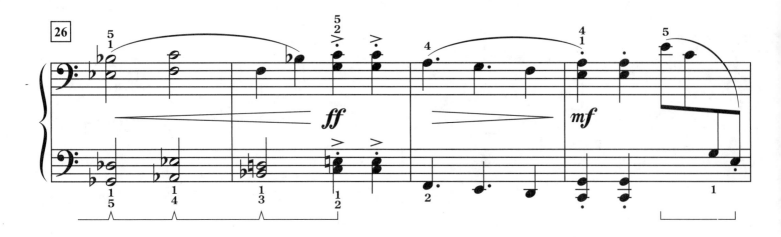

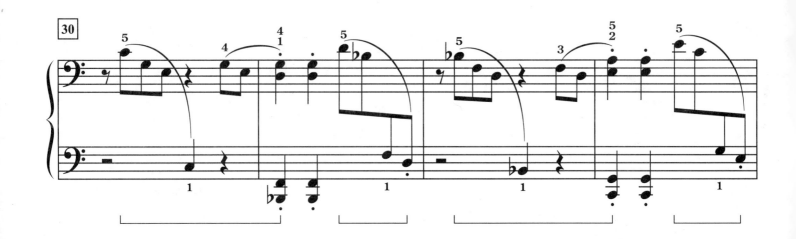

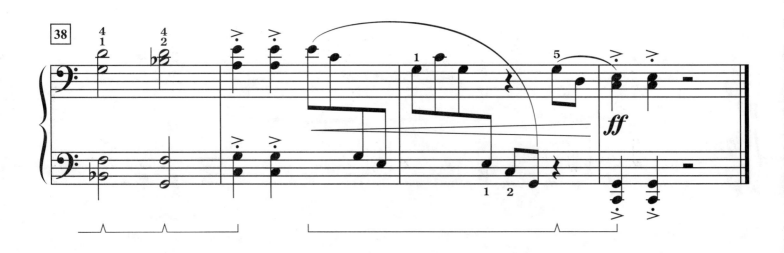

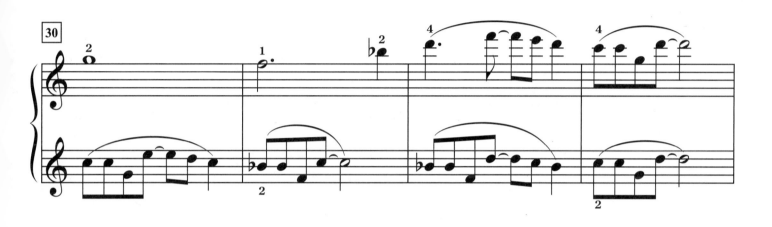